Mother Was a Tragic Girl

CLEVELAND STATE UNIVERSITY POETRY CENTER
NEW POETRY

Michael Dumanis, Series Editor

Samuel Amadon, *The Hartford Book*
John Bradley, *You Don't Know What You Don't Know*
Lily Brown, *Rust or Go Missing*
Elyse Fenton, *Clamor*
Emily Kendal Frey, *The Grief Performance*
Dora Malech, *Say So*
Shane McCrae, *Mule*
Helena Mesa, *Horse Dance Underwater*
Philip Metres, *To See the Earth*
Zach Savich, *The Firestorm*
Sandra Simonds, *Mother Was a Tragic Girl*
S. E. Smith, *I Live in a Hut*
Mathias Svalina, *Destruction Myth*
Allison Titus, *Sum of Every Lost Ship*
Liz Waldner, *Trust*
Allison Benis White, *Self-Portrait with Crayon*
Jon Woodward, *Uncanny Valley*

For a complete listing of titles please visit
www.csuohio.edu/poetrycenter

Mother Was a Tragic Girl

4/2/12

Poems

Sandra Simonds

Cleveland State University Poetry Center
Cleveland, Ohio

ISBN 978-1-880834-96-1

First edition

5   4   3   2   1

This book is published by the Cleveland State University Poetry Center,
2121 Euclid Avenue, Cleveland, Ohio 44115-2214
www.csuohio.edu/poetrycenter and is distributed by
SPD / Small Press Distribution, Inc. www.spdbooks.org.

Cover image: *Into the World There Came a Soul Named Ida* by Ivan Albright,
courtesy of The Art Institute of Chicago.
Mother Was a Tragic Girl was designed and typeset by Amy Freels in Stone Print.

LIBRARY OF CONGRESS CATALOGING-IN-PUBLICATION DATA
Simonds, Sandra, 1977–
Mother was a tragic girl : poems / Sandra Simonds. – 1st ed.
p. cm. – (CSU poetry series) (New poetry)
Includes bibliographical references.
ISBN 978-1-880834-96-1 (acid-free paper)
I. Title.
PS3619.I5627M68 2011
811'.6–dc23

2011042829

Acknowledgments

Many thanks to the editors of the journals where versions of the following poems have appeared.

42Opus	"DuckRabbit"
	"The Battle of Horseshoe Bend"
	"The New Curriculum"
Abraham Lincoln	"I Hate My Life and When I Take Off"
	"Lass, Withdraw Three Hundred Dollars and Get Lost"
American Poetry Review	"1984 Pumpkin Pie"
	"The End of the World"
The Believer	"Wife's Job at the Perpetual Alps Factory"
Black Warrior Review	"'There Is Great Talk of Revolution,' Wife Writes on a Piece of Scratch Paper"
Columbia Poetry Review	"Dear Treatment,"
	"Your Own Winnebago"
Copper Nickel	"A Talented Engraver from Delft"
Court Green	"Advice to My One-Year-Old"
Fence	"Solipsism as Maternal Instinct"
Gulf Coast	"Yoga"
HTMLGIANT	"Strays: A Love Story"
Lana Turner	"Miniature Landscape Made from Green Reykjavik"
Poetry	"Landscape Made from Egg and Sperm"
	"Lines Written on Nursery Wall"
	"You Can't Build a Child"
Puerto del Sol	"Skyhook"

Spooky Boyfriend	"DNA Woven from Lasers in the Jungle"
	"Used White Wife"
Tight	"My Lyric Sensibility Is Gone"

Sincere gratitude to David Kirby and Elaine Treharne. Sincere gratitude to the members (past and present) of my poetry group, who would meet every week to exchange and discuss poems: Frank Giampietro, Vincent Guerra, Rebecca Hazelton, Rebecca Lehmann, and Josephine Yu. Thank you to my friends at Bloof Books: Shanna Compton, Jennifer L. Knox, Anne Boyer, and Danielle Pafunda. Thank you to all of my friends on the PostFlarf Listserv, with special thanks to Maurice Burford and Benjamin Bourlier. Thank you to my Tallahassee girls for their constant love and friendship: Emily Dowd, Stephanie Kennedy, Molly Hand, and Tara Stamm. Also thank you to Mary Biddinger, Michael Dumanis, and Chris Smith, for their attentiveness and care with my manuscript. Special thanks to Barbara Hamby, who helped tremendously with feedback and proofreading at every stage of this book's development. And lastly, thank you to my mother and father, my sister, and Craig.

for Ezekiel Nathan Freeman-Simonds

Contents

Mother Was a Tragic Girl

I.
Beehive

Used White Wife

It is absolutely unnecessary to write serious poetry.
In fact, anyone who even attempts to write
a serious poem reveals him or herself to be
completely anti-intellectual by throwing
his or her brain into a trash heap.

Mao Zedong, your poems are horrible
(especially "Yellow Crane Tower" and specifically
when you state that the "yellow crane is gone,"
and then have the nerve to ask, "Who knows whither?").

My used white wife writes serious poetry
about Jacques Lacan. What a moron!
Doubling the drama of our frequent
disputes, she wraps our newborn son
in the torn pages of his lectures.
She who was rich, she who had beauty,
she who had the advantage of manifesting
symbolic necessity, more purely than Mao Zedong,

wastes her time starting poems with lines like
"That we may believe conception arbitrary,"
as I sit at my workbench, scientific, trying
to manage next spring's gypsy moth population.

Your Own Winnebago

There's a volcano in my Alaska, a Paris
    in my mesa and the bulldog
at the wheel who looks at me with her awful

eyes says, "Sandra, there's no time
    for a vinyasa, so skedaddle," and while
dog paddling to the Eiffel Tower I see

the shenanigans of topography, loop-a-
    doop shooting stars crushed under their own weight,
outrageously obese men and women

strolling down Main Street, happy as
    snapping fingers to the brainstem's want, the penny
slots spitting rednecks as the song goes,

"There's a crater in my Moscow, a hickey
    on my Himalaya, a quicksand pit
on my 9th Tokyo, a Yucatan on this meteor impact

more idiotic than the Patriot Act, more
    ants-in-your-pants than Shays' Rebellion," so drop a few
bouillon cubes in this Mount Everest verb

stew and call it an antsy petroleum,
    the new gold! a wasp that flies
into the vehicle and makes you double over
    the yellow lines for good measure.

A Talented Engraver from Delft

Oh no you're not supposed to fuck your first cousin,
expert on Reform Era pamphlets,
or eat an oatmeal-flavored Powerbar on
the toilet. Even my dog, Milton, knows
not to shit in the room
where you sleep or sleep
where you're not supposed to think of the clitoris

as a velvet curtain
behind which lies a peephole
to the future where
you sit with your colleagues
at the auction of said cousin's
prized possession, *Le Petit Francois*, an engraving
from 1659 with fine hand-colored borders
—even if you lost all of your money,
—even if small portions of the body
are eaten away or there are a few stains
on the leaves of countryside upon which fluffy Italian sheep
have been slowly but surely
munching for over three hundred years
as the rectilinear rays
of sunlight form a little red July house
where you sit on the balcony
amidst a few cherry tomato plants
drinking a Dos Equis.

It is pleasant to receive
an unexpected greeting card
with a three-dimensional stork
outlined in purple glitter

from a twice-removed cousin
in the winter when you grow
cabbage and kale in your garden.
Whatever marginal repairs
which were once so important
seem to slip to the back of your mind as you prepare
to stuff a goose with chestnuts and wine and feed your family
of six who know nothing
of your past at Sotheby's writing half of your poems about
Eurydice on the back
of a Powerbar wrapper and half of them
in the double negatives that cloud the air.

Dear Treatment,

Because I'm the healer of Anglo-Saxon England, before the soul
                             was invented, before
the hematoma on nun's arm, before nun,
      in the enervated sepsis, on intertwined nudes sick with stabs,
            beyond syncope's ventricle-less
vulva, incense simmering, skin undulating in jubilees
          with chipped ghosts, with anxieties
  like *who will be my guide to the next world?*
       I'll tell you to wear a necklace with a gnat
          tied to the end of it to cure a headache;
             I'll tell you to crush pale green flowers with white stone
               to combat flying venom, elfshot,
                  and because I'm the healer I must cut tendons

        to find it, break metacarpals, must
      use the speculum to reach
      the fluted place that this vestigial light is never
allowed to bounce off of, must mix sheep fat
with dust. I contain leechbooks. I contain

    the pre-theologian's instruments, the history of institutions,
      debunked theorems where men and women
        sit and stare as their feet shrink
           to their thighs, waiting for an answer.

I Hate My Life and When I Take Off

all my clothes, mirrors crack
    into a self game of
polyhedral tremors. Self Four says,
"Can't touch the repressed poem with
its suburban address and Dracula cargo
    of sucked flesh." Be-

neath Layer Six are my true feelings: a
Zanzibar of brain shivers
    cut with Xan-
        ax or or-
gasm layer of Florida beach, old lovers
    like historic sperm, synchronized

swimmers folding into self-
deprivation—obsidian
       of sculpted despair where
    I beat the family dog to death
         in a rage over misplaced
     binoculars that I use to
     spy on my sexy neighbor.

"Bury him in a hole in the backyard,"
Self Eight says, "inversely proportional
       to Jupiter's red
       stork bite." I try to tough out

the asparagus urine side effects,
        endure furunculosis (painful nodules
formed in the skin, caused by
bacteria, which enter

through hair follicles),
     a life lacking cliffhangers,
    except these lame self-explosions.

But I want France! I want the
     Med's Bardot breasts! Not
    milkless nipples and sexless sex
     (unless it involves dressing
up like George Eliot), not a bee-

hive frying sausages
   and then piled high
     on a porcelain plate, like Katie's
   mom who died in a mute robe,
    curling her granddaughter's
        limp chicken-noodle hair.

Yoga

From 2007–2009, I did a lot of yoga.
    I was in graduate school and full of hope.
I believed in literature and love.
  Well, maybe I was a little bit cynical.
    It's hard to remember.
I fell in love with someone
    named Craig Wesley Freeman.
Recently, he has told me things that
  I can't recall from the beginning
of our courtship. "This car
    smells like semen and wine,"
he said I said back then.
  He told me that we were both passed
out at a Waffle House and when
  we woke up in the red booth he couldn't
remember where I lived and I couldn't either
  so we drove around Tallahassee
for four hours asking people where
  Sandra Simonds lives and everyone
gave us directions to a different
  Waffle House, which is so inconvenient
and shitty. When we finally got home,
  I wanted to sit in the backyard alone
and look at the pecan tree even though
  it was five a.m. I remember staring
    at a bright celestial body and asking,
  "Jesus H. Christ, is that the sun
or the moon?" and for a split second
  I was so freaked out it made me think
that everyone in my life had died at once
  and I was left alone and that the feeling

of being abandoned was equivalent
   to the feeling of emptiness that
      would make me want to slit
   the throat of a soft pig.

Yoga was incredibly boring.
   My mom called it "stretching."
Over the phone she would ask,
   "Are you going to your
stretching class?" How did
   she get so cynical? The women
who taught yoga were mostly
   beautiful and had Barbie-long arms,
legs, plastic vaginas without holes, and wore
      outfits with suns and moons on them.
They made ordinary looking
   women with soft folds
of fat flesh around the abdomen
   and neck feel bad about themselves so
   what's the deal anyway?
   This too is a kind of cruelty.
They always told us
   about the charity yoga workshops
they taught and "Couldn't we spare
   something, even a smile" to help them?

I resent beautiful women who are flexible
      and talk about Deepak Chopra
   like they're fucking him.
   I resent other things too.
I resent it when people tell me to
   "be like the Buddha."
Hey, fuck you.
   I'll be like the Buddha if I want to.

Lass, Withdraw Three Hundred Dollars and Get Lost

Miss Lux has to piss, but why not write the poem first?
"*Tsk. Tsk.* Eleanor Jones would never write a line like that, Ms. Lux,"
        says Mr. Lux, taking a cooked duck out of the oven.

"Neither would I," says Mrs. Lux, "if it wasn't true."

Bear in mind the disparate energy
        created by the doom force
      of smashing plates on bookshelves as Mr. Lux yells,
"You're a scam artist! You were never a real Wiccan practitioner!"

Suburban Missy Lux bored counting calories.
Superb rhubarb pie, four hundred thirty-six.
      Missus. I miss us, so luxurious.
One quarter of a pecan equals nine.

New Year's Resolutions?

      1. Be more negative
      2. Abuse the dogs
      3. Starve unborn child
      4. Encourage family members to commit suicide

Alternately, Madame Lux behind the wheel of a bigger, badder,
      and better Mademoiselle Lux who buys
        an orange Ferrari, drives it around in a rented tux.

Misanthropic Lux considering gastric
bypass surgery. Hot chocolate, eighty-seven.

O my Luxy Lux,
        I'm going to write the envoi to your poem really quickly
                so that you can move to San Francisco,
        eat dim sum, die alone. So you can
            just get on with it.

No-name Lux, dumb-dumb sans prefix—get your
      dumbbells, make yourself strong, sing

a song or strum while you mow

      Child Lux: Hello, Mr. Smith.
      Mr. Smith: Please, call me Hank.
      Child Lux: Yes, Mr. Smith.

the lawn. For in our world the muon is
heavier than the electron.

Skyhook

Today I lost my mucus plug which
is funny since I'm Kareem Abdul-Jabbar
and did not expect to get pregnant
to begin with. Here are some cool facts you should
probably know before you start sending
my soon-to-be-born son X-mas presents:

My real name is Geraldine Ferraro
and that is the name of the woman who
got me pregnant which means I got myself
pregnant. *Get it?* It all went down
at the Cleveland Clinic in Dayton, Alaska.

I'm also America's first face
transplant and grew up in the town where Robert
Lowell's poem "Skunk Hour" takes place.
Hell yeah, I've seen where that skunk stuck
her snout in sour cream, so steeped in idealism.

FYI, Edgar Allen Poe wrote an excellent
short story on a case of mistaken
identity where the ego creates
and projects itself onto the basket-
ball court which mirrors the political

arena where Ms. Ferraro spent most
of her formative years. But it's Schelling's
concept of "identity" illustrating
the interaction of the individual
with its counterpart, man and machine,
deus ex machina, father and son,
that keeps me going back to the game.

A Warm and Witty Transsexual Prostitute

Alright, Sally. The only thing that will get the sound-
bite of Manuela in Almodovar's *All About my Mother*

crying for her son Esteban out of my head today is
daydreaming about the conference paper I presented on

English trench warfare, wherein I argue that Washington, DC is not a
far-off astrological hub of prepubescent miracle workers with

green skin like most of the literature suggests.
Historians such as Bison T. Carlyle cite that paper now—

(It took some time for them to notice but
jeez, it sure does make me feel pretty darn good).

"Karma's a bitch," Dr. Sally, my academic rival, tells me, and that to
liken my pregnancy to the Russo-Japanese war is a bit

misguided, but I know she's just jealous that I am able to
navigate metaphors such as "trench warfare is the fortification

of the Bollywood film industry like unkissed actors and
prostitutes of West Bengali origin dressed in multicolored

quasar pits stuffed with rosebud wedding cakes the shape and
rigidity of Christopher Columbus's head

some Inuits eat on X-mas." "What?" Sally asks, and I answer like this:

DNA Woven from Lasers in the Jungle

I was at a union party
last year and this girl
was telling me about how her
mom is allergic to everything.
"Everything?" I asked.
"Everything," she replied,
"even the Earth's magnetic field."

❧

I've heard Paul Simon sing
about the boy in the bubble and the baby
with the baboon heart
one too many times today.
(I'm retro like that.)

❧

Have I told you
how his wife's band
drugged my husband
with PCP-laced walnut
cookies about ten
years ago in Dallas
when he was working
as a busboy?

❧

In 1906, French physicist
Bernard Brunhes proved that the earth's
polarity reverses

every so often
by taking warm honey and
pouring it over the
Taung child's (*A. africanus*)
smallish mandible. His parents' life
of seed-gathering, tool-sharpening,
and reproduction is common
in generalized endotherms.
Humans aren't cheetahs,
you know—they don't run
their prey
to the ground. The cost
of bipedal walking:
a bubble allergy.

∾

Dear Jennifer L. Knox:
You've been tellin' me
you're a genius
since you were seventeen
so can you please tell me
why Wislawa Szymborska's poem
"Brueghel's Two Monkeys"
has two monkeys chained
to the floor in
the first stanza? I mean,
is that even possible?

My Lyric Sensibility Is Gone

It's really incredible!
I'm no longer a poet but

a ward, nauseous
when the peroxide halls

fracture to the sound
of nurse shoes on lacquer.

They say genius knows
itself. What a belligerent

mess. The sound of bed
pans in a pigsty. They say the imagina-

tion should be able to con-
trol itself or at least

hold opposite
poles of

thought to-

gether
to make whole but

I'm not Greek stone.
I'm not dried bone.

I can't hold
on to these storm-

white sounds

where clouds
boil earth and

*snow dusts
the skeleton.*

Demolition Psalm

What we should do, my love, is let the rich demolish
the rich, enzyme the catalyst. Let nothing stop
our psychologists' wristwatch checking.

Let our piss hiss to the nuclear metronome,
the goldfish's fission mouth swish for his tail into
the hallucinatory power of endless suck.

Let the dumbest maid ask, "Does tarragon tea
have the power to cure bunions?" Let it be
known, my darling, that dogs have four blood types,

cats eleven, cows around eight hundred. Let Alaska.
No, let Pompeii. And let's not forget to let Botulism cling
to the rim of "you're the last tin can left."

Let our mercury fish apocalypse the heating
oceans, syphilitic and humping. Oh let
elephant AIDS, llama tampons, platypus barf.

Let the fortunate dismantle "The Song of the Humpback Whale,"
metamorphic rock quake the palm's fault lines,
the vaginal canal fill with sparrows.

Instead of Having Your Baby

I'm going to be an ox, a hex-

agon, a hydrogen cell,
a graph without

coordinates. I'm going
to be Blake's chimney for

the sweep, the moccasin's
S across swamp water,

oval of a Moroccan
belly dance.

Not an X. Not brick.
Not a pond.

All the stories
I've ever told are drafts

of bigger lies,
so I'm giving up.

I'm going to be
a trapeze artist.

II.
Strays: A Love Story

Strays: A Love Story

1a.

I don't know why every time she walks the baby
                              down Corinne Street
                    on that black leash, she sees a dead squirrel.
          Nothing unusual. It's all *so* unusual. But this
                    time its brain runs from
mouth—red rivulets. Planets in dirt. She scoops some up, lets Dog
                    eat off her fingers. Wife is
          an intelligent and cultivated young woman.
          Now why does Dog run to Wisconsin, find a
                    horse ranch family with a daughter named
                    Ellena who is fond of *The Italian* by Ann Radcliffe?
                    Daughter Ellena reads to Dog at night.

          Every afternoon Wife's nipples leak titanium as
                    soon as she reads the berserk
          passage in *The Italian*— where Vincentio is acquitted— to young Cashier
                    at the bookstore. How she misses Dog!
                    "I received an email yesterday in which I was instructed to
                              register for a website and then email fifteen people the cure for
                              sickle cell anemia within the next two hours or
                              it said I would die," she tells Cashier.

                    Moreover, she is frightened.
                    Each night she thinks,
                              Answer.
                    No one. *Answer.*
                    Her beauty: it's a carbon copy of squirrel eyes, an unearthed
                              Etruscan vase if it breaks

down the middle and you trace the zebra fissures
on its surface with your forefinger.
Easy to say, "Dog runs to Wisconsin."
Someone say *something*. My books.
Not one person
on this planet is going
to buy my handmade books.

1b.

Tipsy Wife in love with young Cashier,
(here's to you). You decide not to send any
emails because it's your death and you don't

care to be bullied into it.
Onward!
Now Mother calls.
Terrible timing.
Excuse the mess.
"Tipsy. I'm tipsy. No I'm drunk on mint juleps and Dog

is missing," you tell Mother.

Her answer? "Dog was unpleasant and
I know you know he shit all over the house."

Stars in Wisconsin
tumble over
one another until they are ground down, until they
ring out
yesterday's fine sulfurous powder.

2a.

And then Cashier begins to
        catch on to Wife's advances.
                Oh really?
        Zeroing in on that cut forefinger
                yelp has never been his
            game of choice. He doesn't want to give away that he is in high school,
and that he is bullied and has recently thought about hanging himself with a thin breeze.
                "My chances of dying each day" he googles, and the first thing that comes up?
                Ellena has a 26/6,000,000,000 chance of dying from a shark attack.

2b.

Tonight he roams the aisles of CVS looking for. . . . *aha . . .*
high potency acne medication. Tonight he puts that medication
 in his trench coat and walks out wanting
            nothing less than to get caught. *Catch me if you can.*

Give up, Wife thinks, on her evening walk. Wife
sees Sparrow flying from
            a newspaper mailbox.
      Light Sparrow carries away an article about a cold case in which a
      thirteen-year-old girl was raped and run over
                  eight times with a truck.
      Rick Bass, the cop, says there's no way the crime was committed by one person.

            She imagines Sparrow
                        understands sorrow but when Sparrow smashes its head
                  right into another sparrow in a freak mid-air sparrow accident,
                              really, she can feel
                                    only remorse for her imagination.

Until now Husband spends most of his time in the meat shop,
            nursing a cold. He has been mute since April of last year,
deaf since the age of fourteen. He has had

enough of Wife's odd behavior. Tonight he brings home a
            donkey and a lamb. "There's a starfish in the lamb's coat just
beyond his head," says Wife.
            "Yes there is," Husband confirms. "A
                  depth catches me," she says and as

easily as saying it she
pulls out the starfish which
         turns black like carbon.
    "Hush," it says.

3a.

When Dog writes Wife a letter which begins, "You had better watch
        out," and ends with
                "Long gone. My best wishes,
                        Very Novemberly,
(enclosed with a howl),
        signed, sealed, delivered, your former loyal canine . . . Milton,"

        Milton does not bark. He explains how life on the farm suits
                a dog more than life in suburbia and how angry he is that the yucky,
                yellow baby has upstaged him.

Husband has never cared for Dog but is happy to know that he
        uses his time so wisely with his new family. *Dog's letters are
                        never enough*, Wife thinks, and falls asleep.

        Time-stamped. Amorphous. There is no return address.

3b.

O Wife, you hypochondriac! Heart beating too fast, chest
wheezing, baking-soda-pale skin.

Establish disease, seek
instant fixes,
        medical advice,
poison for your winding staircase night terrors, gastroenteritis, fingernail loss, rabies? leprosy?

O Wife, get the doctor to prescribe
Valium or an antidepressant that boosts several neurotransmitters. How they fire!

Eerie is the fungal brain. Brain, O Wife, is a front.

Rice. Wheat. Gum. Ban them from your diet.
        I want you to try this free-range donkey meat for your backache.
            Should you shiver,
        hold a cube of ice to your forehead and recite Psalm 23.
                Eat only fermented organic figs mixed with that donkey's ear-tips.
                    Don't bathe in anything but mochi and millet. The brain's Western Front.

4.

To say Wife misses Dog like a parrot misses its clipped, talkative wings would be an understatement.
        Hold on. Cashier and Wife have made love in the bathroom at the bookstore.
Ear parts uncurl: it's creepy but pleasant. Hold on. It's a rainbow sprinkled donut.

She might get arrested like those high school teachers on *America's Most Wanted.*
        Kiss skull. It freaks her out but not enough to change anything. Cashier has to

    unearth *The Italian* from the squirrel eye dirt, then go to band practice.

    Lonely Wife doesn't ask what instrument he plays. Kiss skull, skin fool.
    Loony Wife imagines the drums or the saxophone?

Sixteen years and her son will be as old as Cashier; human life is Jell-O and bones.

Poor Cashier plays the flute and has lied about band practice.
        In fact, today he must find the right medicine for his acne.

Nice pharmacist discussing the pill with a girl from his school. Cashier wants a tattoo that
says "Peace on Earth" in Chinese symbols written across his pelvis.

5a.

My world is shaped like a palm frond, thinks Husband. He knows it is
        oblong, a malady of sharp bird
trills. It is angina. And it's damned impossible to titrate enough

hot plant scent from the cumulonimbus clouds to make a perfume for her.
        Egg life. In wait.
           Rich cholesterol cures he

  will not invent in time, so how will he get her back?

    And the idea, of course, is to grow meat on trees—to grow

steak, ribs, soup bones with
        a deep mahogany marrow, drumsticks, wings.

        Timing. It's all about timing.

    Right away,
        after work, he toils with
giants in his lavender-walled laboratory, reads the letters of Pierre La Monke,
        18th-century alchemist.

        Come on, onyx, you're on to something!

    Gust of eyes: It begins to rain orange robes
in Wisconsin where Dog helps the other displaced monks build a shrine, offer
    raisins at the foot of a statue of a god with fifty heads.

    Look here, Husband. Does a donkey shank grow from that oriental-fan bonsai spruce?

Crazy Husband reads La Monke's sixth letter:

"Heaven's metals must be understood
only backwards. But that makes one forget 'to
kindle' means 'to be molten forward.'
Every time one ponders this,
one comes to see that meat's
never-ending existence is a for-
ward plant. For at no moment, will you find
origin, *i.e.* the right cauldron. Vowels
rise. White plants are scrubbed,
denatured; Pupil, observe backward
signs in the sunrise."

6.

Then Wife begins to sleep with her son's *uh oh* Pediatrician.
        Washed out waiting room. Two mothers exchange stories of their

irritating children who battle ADHD.

        Sit still. Uh oh, the kids spill their candies all over the white
            tile floor. They roll, scatter,
                    ignite. Wife begins to wonder:
Now, am I cheating on *uh oh* Cashier, Husband or Pediatrician?

        Go away, mothers.

The Pediatrician, dull as lowfat yogurt, never talks about alchemy like
        Husband or Albert Camus's
            ethical imperative like Cashier, but when he cries,
                "Never let me go, Dog," after they have sex with
        each other in one of the examining rooms
while Baby is crawling around, considering all that has happened with
        Milton's departure, in an
           odd way, it endears Wife to Pediatrician. Wife always leaves the office,
        underwear twisted, hair smelling metallic like rain.

        Tonight she writes a book called "The History of Analytic Geometry."
        Her first line? "Mighty are these *uh oh* numbers, joined with art like iron rods."

7a.

Tuesday, C is rushed to the Emergency Room where doctors Jim and Jack (J&J) pump
out his stomach and remove the nine pictures of S that
C has stapled to various places on his body including his foreskin because
on Monday S rejected his friend invitation on Facebook, so psychiatrist P recommends
Moahtadol (a drug well-known for its suicidality risk in teens) but not before C confesses to his
elderly G that he has been sleeping with W, so a Wife Warrant (WW) is sent
out for her arrest while C spends the next week recovering at home taking Moahtadol, while dreams of
umbilical cords interrupt his orgasm via masturbation, but since he is on M,
time is stone, in close quarters, gargantuan, of bent seas, like carved gargoyle teeth,—oh how he
suffers from intrusive thoughts of chopping up S with a butter knife
and fork purring, *come out safe, S,* as he places her under the fake
floorboards of his clapboard house like he read in a posthumously published
Edgar Allen Poe story titled "Come Out Safe" in English class in 9th grade with S by his side.

7b.

Sunday, Wife is arrested by an enormous lesbian cop the size and shape of a
        used Gertrude Stein. "Before the flowers of friendship faded, friendship faded,"
                Nancy recites, instead of reading Wife her Miranda rights.

        Four days later Cashier kills himself, leaving a rambling note
of oblong proportions: a paranoid delusion that his mother and S are involved in a
        relationship based on the ethical principles of Albert Camus. Our forever-sunny,

easygoing Pediatrician begins to have sex with
        Victoria, one of the mothers of the *uh oh* children with ADHD.

        Enormous Nancy was the other mother. Is that
right? Writer wrong. He does not call her "Dog." He calls her "Mom."

8.

Writer gives Baby her cell phone.
        How do I distract him so that I can have
                eleven more minutes to write? she thinks.
Now something sad happens and the story is
        momentarily swept up, like the mahogany floor of
                your neighbor's cute Victorian house.
Mother's story is like a wooden skull because it creaks.
Or her story isn't like a wooden skull because it will not crack.
        Tick-tock Writer must breastfeed Baby,
        has to change his mushy diaper and
even though she feels that her own story has betrayed her,
                rented out its own house, she is not sure what she can
                        do about this.

In the other room, Baby calls Hunan Province and spends
        eleven minutes on the phone with the
        distracted manager of a factory that makes
                iPhones and battery-operated stuffed bears
                who wear Ralph Lauren suits
                and plastic monocles and
                        sing "Hound Dog"
                very happily when you turn them on.

Yes, Baby smiles for the first time, turns his head to his
only love, says, "I embrace the horror of being virgin."

"You must tell me what Baby said on the phone to rack up a
nine-hundred dollar bill," Wife says to the phone company.

        "Give me all your bears." Over and over.

9.

Tired Husband flies to Wisconsin in an attempt to bring back
his pet, which he thinks will restore his relationship with Wife.

Eight days before, the media comes to his door, asks
dumb but daring questions about Wife. He answers,
"I cannot discuss the case because I am a mute alchemist."
     Very well. (No one says that.) "Also, I am deaf."

In no time, he finds Milton, fluffy terrier blessed with insight,
next to Ellena, on the ranch. She is reading him *The Italian*:

"Esteemed Vivaldi was the divine image of interiority.
In his castle he asked himself . . . Can this be human nature,
most horrible perversion of right? Can man, that most puzzling
ape, endowed with reason, argue himself into the commission of such
gigantic folly, such inveterate cruelty, as exceeds all the acts of
even the most irrational and ferocious brute?"

10.

Some mute things.
    Or rotten meat.
        Or analytic geometry.
        Time for prion diseases; time to make love to the flu.

        Cannot forget the sexual fantasies that involve George Eliot.
           A 2012 study which concludes that

neighborhood squirrel deaths are attributable to
nano amounts of antidepressants infiltrating the groundwater.

One long bout of dissociative fugue can be cured if you
        trust Writer to rename it *pilgrimage*.

Sometime after it is renamed, Writer becomes an ambiguous figure.

Poor thing. Wife's not really in jail.
        Or Writer might become Dog or Wife.

In one story, Wife is renamed *gradual*.
        Listen, *gradual* might be renamed *George Eliot*, *Husband*, or *Dog*.

You have to understand: everything here dazzled them.

Or Wife is not merely a guest of the forest but is master

    until Writer is master of Dog who
        realizes Dog is master of Husband who realizes Husband is master only
           when Cashier is the master of red meat.

Husband is searching for an adventure
        inside marvel.

Thanks to this eerie magic, Wisconsin, and the most beautiful
          hardwood oak shaped by nature
and science under which he has found Dog longing for the

          inside of the pantry in the house where Wife keeps
                    rat-shaped biscuits.

11.

Mother was a tragic girl who
     I think about every day, thinks Pediatrician between patients.
           Never choke on words, she choked on words, never
       discard a scratched thing; she discarded her own life, the linoleum
              sun, twisting and twisting forever.
         So this is why I am what I do,
               twisting the new mouth, prescribing. I love Wife's
                      risks, wrists,
                    uterus, underwear, and the structure of our
              cozy game, how it alters,
                    tears, surrounded by a depth, an
             untrue depth. Mother was a tragic girl,
        roped to her context: washing porcelain dishes with painted roses.
           Even though she'll never come out safe,
        by this I do not mean she despaired,
     unless, of course, I despair. I mean
         things alter. Mother said wolves hunt but man is
           not like his monkey skull.
           O impoverished bone,
           time spins inside your
              hard case, spins wolf red,
              inverts red until it becomes a yelp.
          No, a howl. There where the sun implodes. Please
            go, mind, structure, tragic girl.

12.

Because it is impossible to fully comprehend the no/
   yes intricacies that entwine beast and man,
          syrup and powder,
              cyborg and Frankenstein mask,
                  reward and doing the right thing, Dog returns home with Husband, without
                        a care, claws clipped, lounges in the 1970s
torn, crushed-velvet easy
chair, alternately reading to Baby,
        "Holy one, rescue me from this bad pass and guide me towards some inhabited place," and
               eating a dog bone Husband has finally grown from an oak.

              Dog scratches his head of fleas, removes a few
      ticks from his abdomen. How he enjoys the orange evenings of October, un-
      hinged, dotted with leaves—crisp, veined, these
              inside the house things, scratched things, that roam, leave, turn
                      normal into nomad and then turn to
                gone, gnawing on marrow, ice cream,
          snowing leaves, now snarling—with Wife, Husband, Baby.

III.
Made from Scratch

The End of the World

No, not the apocalypse of Dante's imagining, rather,
    stamp collecting, the philatelic   investment of
my father. Just heaping piles of   licked stamps,
curved edge   of the January Mediterranean if you

rotate it ninety degrees. Stamps!
    Stamps!   hovering over Siberia!
crisscrossing Mongolia!   Carbon snowflakes!
    Square-inch stories   thrown out of an airplane
over the Mojave!   Stamps pounding like hooves!
Steam engine of a locomotive! Guatemala!   My fetus's
quadruple heart rate! They make

their way to Eli Frank in Easton, Maryland,
    seller of thimbles,   bubble wrap,   q-tips,   toilet paper,
anything and everything, but,   above all,
stamps: the pastel heads of   overthrown leaders,
    landscape of palms and figs, Elvis, flags of extinct
nations   ruffling in the revolutionary   wind and then
    falling from   the metal scoop Eli held
into the Ziplock bag that I held

open thereby   confirming the final journey
    of the paper gazelles of Chad,   rose sands
of Mogadishu,   Picasso's weeping women,
    the stylish cafés of Sarajevo   in one of the only
moments when my   father and I shared
a common purpose,   to touch the thin earth's crust
—to place the stamp   in the right spot
    in the stamp book. These uprooted images,
now side by side,   in rows: how terrible   that King Tut
    could not   protest   having   to stay put.

Barrier Reef

Hold a marble's internal structure, its glass math
    as close as you can to your right iris, watch the trapped
cataract swirl then bisect your eye the way
      school children dissect a cow's eye. Then put it up
to your mouth, put your tongue to the red meat zinc,
      the mirror's mirror.
    Get closer to the innards of glass,
    clots, potassium, organelles, appendix,
     just before it bursts with universe.
        Blood's the word. Gut hot.

The surface of the mind is words,
        wounds, worlds, its gold
skin bulges when there's too much bacteria
    in it, too many life forms to fit
        or ax the ordinary skull just to see
what's inside: the parrot fish's horny
      beak and four molars
set deep in its throat, the satyr-colored

king coral. The Fins! Flippers! Rays, Rings!
      So much trapped, as if
      always looking through colored
glass gardens congealed in stone—Spires!
    and Stems! Fans! and Fronds!
      Still, the sea grows and grows:
      a gate opens the glasswork of bone.

The Battle of Horseshoe Bend

I was going to write a poem about giving birth,
          about meconium, vernix,
                    the cubic zirconium
          scattered on the floor tiles of the hospital room.
          It would have been about false
                    windows that face false
          walls, about
          the tiny hamburger I ate afterward
—the mustard too yellow and sweet—the flushed

cheek of labor, how hard it is
          to piss afterwards, how hard it is just to walk
                    to the bathroom. Not that ward. Not that one.

          And it was going to be about my son,
                    the military history of America.
          That it would have erased
          all mothers is of no
          consequence. That it would have fought
          for the common defense
     is of no consequence. That it would embrace
                    the cyclonic energy of

          Andrew Jackson would have only been
                    a byproduct.

     Instead, it will be about some Choctaw Indians,
          some Jews, about government cheese, debt, rent, some

     steam off the Georgia swamp on my way
          to work at six a.m., where the egret transfixes the grass,
                    the chocolate dark pines of the New World.

That it would have had to murder the landowner
in the name of personal property, resign before it

takes office, retract its oath, X out
its flight path like a bird of prey.
There is no
consequence.

Poem of trading posts, missions, forts,
garden plots, the Sand Grain Plantation,
where you can pretend to be a pilgrim
or an Indian, a landowner or a slave.
Poem that erases itself as it is written.
Poem that will never exist.

1984 Pumpkin Pie

Even on their totally awesome chestnut-colored horses,
      the Indians were fucked over and we knew it
so anyone who was anyone in the third grade
      wasn't going to be caught dead in an Albertson's
paper bag cut down the middle, decorated
      in red and yellow crayon "pictographs," worn
as an Indian vest for the Thanksgiving Festival
      at Center Street School in El Segundo, CA,
where, before 1934, there were four signs on the cardinal
      points of town that read:
      "No Blacks, No Jews, No Dogs."

No question that when she chose me to be an Indian, I felt
      a John Wayne wild sense of betrayal
by Mrs. Trachtenburg, who could have easily turned
      me into a pilgrim, like Kristen with her Norwegian
blonde hair, making me wear a paper-towel
      white hat, simply by saying,
"Sandra Simonds, you will be a pilgrim."

I colored my vest along with Julie,
      who worked so hard in school, who everyone called
a "retard," who had had a stroke
      in the womb, who I thanked god
was a Christian because she would have never
      made it through Hebrew School. Everyone
was nice to her only because they knew
      that, at the drop of that pilgrim's hat, they could be mean.

      My Indian name was Careful Dove,
    because the class called me Butterfingers.

Little bespectacled Indian Jew—*Schlemiel*—
        on a horse—fighting the white man,
            at the Festival, in front of our parents.

    We recited our Indian poems. Careful Dove
            said each line while Julie drooled:

Peaceful dove. Alone.
Fly around the town.
Oy vey! Careful Dove. Alone.
Eat a pumpkin pie when you get home.

Then all of us pilgrims and Indians took
            out our recorders (because the music
        teacher had to fit a performance into the
        curriculum) and played "Love Me Tender."
Even Julie, who couldn't play a C, pulled
        a plastic recorder out of her paper vest.
We were told to play in unison but
        we sounded like geese, lost in our own flock.

DuckRabbit

This is the story of my grandfather Benjamin Levy
      who survived Auschwitz. He wrote his biography on
        a torn label of a can of con-
                  densed milk. He took dictation. He
          dictated. He flipped the dialectic, threw that scrap in the air.
          It landed on the other
       side of history. People think prisoners
               don't gamble.
      Gamblers are always and only prisoners. Lucky
             bastard. Once he told me that the spine is a prison.
         To gamble, he said, you need to lose
             your spine.

The following is a translation into English of that scrap
found by his wife of over fifty years, Suzanne Levy:

"November 8, 1944.

      Background works at sawing off my right foot, my foot
          a growling ground down
             to bits of Timbuktu. It is full of sun, this slit into the out
             there. *Duckrabbit*
          duckrabbit duckrabbit. Into is so bright it will make
        you vomit. I am the figure, a screwed
figment, a reckoning shade, life's filaments, spare
        time's one statement called 'once upon.' I've been working
          on my tunnel
      vision morphing portals lined with dried corn."

      Can you believe that's his whole life story?
      Can you believe that's the other side of history?

Arnold Chanin, his grandson (who also happens to be
a corrections officer in Macon, Georgia, and the "I" of this poem)
decides to decode this scrap.

He/I spend/s many nights
                in the attic where the scrap
            landed after it was thrown in the air. History's drafty.
                He/ I tap/s into his dictation. It is dusty.
                        He/I dictate/s. There is a fine lavender
                    powder that sits on the scrap. People think poets
                    don't gamble. Poets are always
                        and only gamblers.

The following is the final interpretation of the scrap
by Arnold Chanin, author of this poem:

"November 8, 1988.

            Across from Auschwitz they are building a mall. Upon entering the mall
                        trees form completely
            from the air-conditioning system. Perchance you'll purchase a
                        Duckrabbit duckrabbit duckrabbit?
                I was screwing around with the century's broken
                links when, all of the sudden,
                        because man can only be one
                animal at a time and because one animal
                        can only be two men
                at a time and because two monkeys are
                chained to the floor of this attic
                        with evolutionary thoughts running
                beneath their craniums, and because we take one eye
                        from an animal and one
                                eye from man, I was ordered to build
                        a figure who recedes into the ground

down background
from the ousted queen's crown,
the drowned neck of a Nazi named
Heimlich, a can of condensed milk,
and dried ears of corn."

The New Curriculum

is all about showing off how different it will be from
      the old curriculum. The old
                     books pointing us to the new
        ones won't matter when the old
ones point us to the
      new. You, the new you,
         will learn one
less language. This situation is like looking into the purple eyes
        of a beautiful woman only to find
             that she is a seal, lives in the ocean,
       dreams about sardines (if, of course, seals
eat sardines) and though kelp may sway
          her body, that seal won't have anything
      to do with you, the old curriculum.
    No more turning
    a turducken into a kiwi fruit, a koala bear into
          cayenne pepper, a conquistador into
      confectioner's sugar. Dim-
inutive fantasy, this is common
     sense. No crème brûlée. It's all
      russet potato here.

     Pretend that holes
in maps look through nowhere and go
     from there. Go
     north for winter. Do not
     suffer through ice (technically
       a mineral). Take a protractor
        and compass and mark exactly
       where you are with a large
         red X. You are one
          step less.
         Replace. Replace.

You Can't Build a Child

with the medicinal poppies of June
nor with Celan's bloom-fest of dredged stone,
         not with history's choo-choo train of corpses
(like the Jew I am), not with Nottingham's Robin Hood
            nor Antwerp's Diamondland.

Not walking on The Strand in Manhattan Beach with her
      silicone breast implants, refinery, waves of trash,
            not out of the Library of Alexandria
         with her burnt gardens that prefigure
gnarly, barnacle-laden surfboards broken in half.

You can't build a child with the stone paths
         that we have walked on through the atmosphere,
            the pirate's plank, the diving board, the plunge,
         nor with the moon whether
            she be zombie or vampire.
      Not with Delphi, not with fangs, or cardamom bought
         in Fez, red with spring, red with
               marathon-running cheeks.

      Not with monk chant, bomb chant,
   war paint, not with the gigantic Zen pleasure zones,
            nor with the harnessed pig
on this carrousel that I am sitting on with my son
         in Nice, France. How it burns on its axis
      as if it were turning into pineapple-colored kerosene
the way the Hawaiian pig, apple in snout, roasts
            in its own tropical meat under the countdown sun.

"There Is Great Talk of Revolution," Wife Writes on a Piece of Scratch Paper

"ha.   ha.   ha," she laughs.

                                      ~

But when she thinks about what it means
    to live in this world, this mischief ghost,
        red as an emergency appendectomy, she longs
    to be a jet-set ambassador who brings back
          a mini basalt salt cellar
from a wrinkled landscape, the brain,
          —Bulgaria—.

When she's in her apartment she imagines how ghosts crisscross Earth's
    curvature, how Falun Gong practitioners are killed for organ harvest,
      how innovative physics teachers prep for class, how
    the Earth's ground-
      water is as gray as larva swept
in the veins of the sick and how,
  at this moment,
 some tapeworm, astonishing thing, is teeth-
ing a system of
sun and stars with its para-
    sitic twirling.

But then she leaves her place, faces traffic,
      goes out to eat,
      orders shawarma (امرواش),
    meets her friend, Sister Hope,
      tells her that every
          day she tastes odd
  toxins, tastes her whole life's post-
mortem apparition marked by dents.

Wife's Job at the Perpetual Alps Factory

I work in the BLACK HOLE wing outside Bern (on a machine
that looks like a spinning jenny) placing umlauts over

the a's in *war* to turn them to *were*, which is why we who war
translate German into *we* were. I'm all for planetary annihilation,

all for pulling the big red umlaut-lever
down to make the final BLACK HOLE. Don't like your house?

Don't like your face transplant, calf implants, husband, dog?
Well, compress the pomposity of your visionary despair

into a facet of being more humorous: Imagine two
standard poodles walking down Obergoldback Straße in baby blue

sweaters with hanging pompoms, hand-knit by their grandmother.
Don't like your shabby address? Here I am ready, set to solve

your shanty town problem so far from these Swiss bank accounts,
so far from the safe where my boss keeps *The Potato Eaters*

and her frozen eggs. All she has to do is whisper
sarcophagus and then our life saga will zilch the iceberg, will smell

of negative sage, will be neither freeze nor thaw, mummy
nor scarab pendant. Minus frenzy. Plus zoo. Minus Sinai wandering.

Solipsism as Maternal Instinct

For a while, everyone loved me.
I got so confident that I put magenta high-
      lights in my mane. There was even a little
    sway to my gait. My hips
grew fuller and I considered
      myself beautiful. I beautified
the displaced space around my
      form the way a mare bends
    the landscape. I wore less
clothes, allowed my breasts
    a bit of sunlight and then I nursed
my child in public. It was like my body
was one big eye, opening and shutting.

For a while, everyone asked me how
my baby was doing, about my plans
for the future. I had
      friends. Once in a while one of them
would say, "Oh let me get that," and
take some cash out of her wallet
      and buy me coffee.

How was I supposed to know I was a cyclops,
      that the opening and shutting
    was because there was powdered milk
caught behind my contact lenses,
      that people were still talking about
    men I had sex with years ago?

Then my milk dried up. My husband
      failed his paternity
        test and left. (We have not seen him since

July 18th, 2009, so if anyone
        knows where he is, please
email me. $200 reward.) Then all my friends
        followed suit, like Annie who
            who left a note on my doorstep
            that said "Can you
please return my DVD of *Beaches*
            and those Onesies I gave
            you. I'm pregnant again."

My son jumps up and down in the second-
        hand Exersaucer that I've set up in
            the living room.
                        The air is composed
            of beaks and hooves, squawks,
                    neighs, unraveling DNA.
        "You're brilliant," these plastic
        farm animals say, their primary colors
            made in God's image.

Advice to My One-Year-Old

If it ends up that you are gay, please try to
         be fabulous, okay?
(*i.e.* beauty, beauty, beauty?)
Go to New York City often and find
         gorgeous men who enjoy fucking,
              drinking, and Schubert. The three
                  go together very well.

I prefer that you
don't end up living in Encino like
         my friends John and Jeff
spending their only
     day off discussing
         what color they should paint their
master bedroom because if you
         do then you might as well be
              a straight woman living a gay man's
                  existence, which doesn't
sound like a lot of fun.
         Who would want to apron their life?

         But, if that is what you choose, then
         you'll need to be a good chooser:
         Find someone who
     wants to cheat on you but doesn't because
                  this will prove
that he has vitality but channels it.
         Find someone who won't leave
              strings of used dental floss
         in the bathtub (like your father).
                  Find someone who will learn

to paint later in life
because he wants to see you
in every way possible. Find someone
who likes to rock
Los Angeles to sleep.
Use a condom, please.

Ah Little Ezekiel,
I wasn't born a Jewish mother
for nothing.

Lines Written on Nursery Wall

You bring a stalk of bamboo
            to the flu room.
                Hot pink Buddha offers
        some bullet-like pills from his plastic
fingers. Oh high above the pecan
tree, my dead grandfather
        walks Basil and Maestro, our two
standard poodles. One's beard is oily
        from the wheel
of Brie he's stolen from
the kitchen counter.

        The world works. Even from here.
                I can hear the buzz
                of machines, the clicks
                        of pens, the secretary's
                                repressed anger
                                (bites the inside of her cheek),
                the weird light of computer screens.

        The world works
                wonders: the cashier at
                    Kmart rings up
                another self-tanning lotion. She rings
                        up August, the ocean, a string
                            bikini on younger flesh. Nude on bronze.
                        Saltwater fish.

        The sand is piled high.
                It makes a wave over the pecan tree.
                Soon a tsunami will wash away
                            the house, nursery.

Nothing left but a palm frond,
white long-bone.

Goodbye dog, tree, grandfather
with your elk-tipped cane.

The world works
but not today. Not for me. Fever and the walls
painted with sharks and starfish.

There is so much aqua, histamine.

Buddha, bring me another
slice of pineapple.

Fairytale Landscape Made from the Leak

Something leaks from my ceiling
     turns to a tea-stained map of Listertown
       where the flesh of its citizens
is covered with toxic drywall
       imported from a rogue nation
      whose Pear Tree Exhibit
      we once visited and admired
    in the mellow month of Tune our
family scrubbed the
    walls of a June
no one can recall.

La la la people in debt,
La la la those who flee,
the disappeared, and many lali lali winters
    when we eat Vaselinebread
that makes us lose our fingernails.
Meat, we grow from black fungus,
    and we slurp up nightmares with
our clear soup. "All speech
here tastes of onion and flu,"

Pregnant Cass coos to her
      February bedmate.
   He sucks his thumb.
    Cass wears a pigeon's nest hat
    and this morning when she cracked
some eggs to make an omelet—poof—
powder poured all over the pan-
demic here, a pandemic air.

Under the boxspring lives
    Toddler Toes—all duct, all node.
    Every night he goes out
to set fire to the map; and then the map
        growss back.
    Toes dozes off, then
    plays with mommy's hat, sings

Lo lo lo. Nobody's home.
Ash floats above
    Cass's naval, her skin stretched

blue to meet the needs
    of the unborn woe.

    And then the map grows back.
    The leak is full of baby fat.

Miniature Landscape Made from Green Reykjavik

I raw ice.
I biked
slice meaning
Plane crash in Lockerbie,
to absolute
What a mess

Which is a frictionless
where molecules
gravity. (That's what
When the Swiss smoke
is a fat farm Anglo girl

How I wanted
That's when I broke
and a gecko and a
See how the proprietress
with her crisscross
calcifies Christmastime

a shoehorn,
a woman's molar
one side of the equal
the dismantling of lamps

I war, ci?
on an ice
"warlice chic," oui?
Scotland: -273 degrees
zero is anyone's guess.
of birthmarks.

variety of Moroccan Mint
mash and helium defies
the buried mammoth ate).
twirls her curls
with smallpox less cows and so on.

to be blonde!
into the Christian farmhouse
gecko and a gecko.
scoops eyeballs from skulls
ladle? What a rustic song
inside a crate with Adorno,

a miniature chateau,
and Kafka's sisters yodeling
sign isn't necessarily equal to
or subjects on the other, a gate.

Landscape Made from Egg and Sperm

Because Yosemite's high altitude lakes'
           tadpoles wash up in
                      glow-in-the-dark condoms
     and every fish lip has a hook in it. Because
                      there's birdshit
                      in the clouds. Things
           catch, get caught. Things
                      are consumed.
                      There's no looking
                                 back. And so you

                      were conceived here, Ezekiel, fifty
           feet off the Trail of
        Broken Ankles. We wanted
to make sure no one
           would see. The one hiker
                      who saw
           looked away.
                      Amino acids
                      of the flushed cheek. Dirge
                                 for eyeless things. I washed
                                 my body in the river
                                            and the river went numb—
                                 the mind sunburnt.

                      I imagine the second
           before you took, before
           the cells began to split,
                      before that flint
        was struck, before the DNA
                      began to twist,

that a colorless emptiness
suddenly inverted
and told the world that, he too,
once had a mother.

But there is
no nest of leaves. Nothing
stops. The clock in the glacier
still ticks above us

and on our skin
there were enormous ants, the segments
of their bodies
like black droplets of paint
pushed very close against each other
but still not touching, yet

taking their work with them—
taking away their dirt world.

Notes

"Yellow Crane Tower," referenced in the poem "Used White Wife," is a poem by Mao Zedong.

In "A Talented Engraver from Delft," *Le Petit Francois* is a 17th-century engraving that appeared in a Christie's auction catalogue.

In "Dear Treatment," the poem references medical practices of Anglo-Saxon England. It was thought that making a necklace with a fly or gnat tied to the end of it would cure certain diseases. In Anglo-Saxon folklore, "Elfshot" refers to a person being attacked by the invisible arrow from an elf. The consequence of such an attack would render its victim ill.

In "Lass, Withdraw Three Hundred Dollars and Get Lost," a muon is an elementary particle similar to an electron.

In "My Lyric Sensibility Is Gone," the line "snow dusts the skeleton" is from Paul Celan.

In "DNA Woven from Lasers in the Jungle," the lines "You've been tellin' me you're a genius since you were seventeen" are from Steely Dan.

In the eighth section of "Strays: A Love Story," the line "I embrace the horror of being virgin" is from Stéphane Mallarmé.

In the ninth section of "Strays: A Love Story," lines at the end of the section are adapted from Ann Radcliffe's novel *The Italian*.

A Note on the Form of "Strays: A Love Story"

Most of the parts of this poem are acrostics using lines from the poet George Oppen. The other parts (parts 7b-10) are acrostics using lines from William Blake. The first letter of each line corresponds with each letter in the Blake or Oppen line. The following lines are used from George Oppen or William Blake's poems:

Part 1a: "I don't mean he despairs, I mean he does not"
Part 1b: "The context is history"
Part 2a: "A cozy game"
Part 2b: "Things alter, surrounded by a depth"
Part 3a: "Wolves may hunt"
Part 3b: "O we impoverished"
Part 4: "The skull spins"
Part 5a: "Mother was a tragic girl"
Part 5b: "Choke on words"
Part 6: "Twisting the new mouth"
Part 7a: "To come out safe"
Part 7b: "Sun forever"
Part 8: "When my mother died, I was very young"
Part 9: "The divine image"
Part 10: "Soot cannot spoil your white hair"
Part 11: "Mind's structure, but nothing"
Part 12: "By scratched things"